ANCIENT GREECE

BY DIANE BAILEY

Essential Library

An Imprint of Abdo Publishing | www.abdopublishing.com

ANCIENT GREECE

BY DIANE BAILEY

CONTENT CONSULTANT

Jonathan M. Hall
Phyllis Fay Horton Distinguished Service Professor in the Humanities
Professor, Departments of History and Classics, and the College
The University of Chicago

www.abdopublishing.com

Published by Abdo Publishing, a division of ABDO, PO Box 398166, Minneapolis, Minnesota 55439.
Copyright © 2015 by Abdo Consulting Group, Inc. International copyrights reserved in all countries.
No part of this book may be reproduced in any form without written permission from the publisher.
Essential Library™ is a trademark and logo of Abdo Publishing.

Printed in the United States of America, North Mankato, Minnesota

102014
012015

THIS BOOK CONTAINS
RECYCLED MATERIALS

Cover Photos: Leemage/Corbis, foreground; Shutterstock Images, background

Interior Photos: iStock/Thinkstock, 6–7, 10 (background), 14–15, 97; Red Line Editorial, 10 (inset),
59; Nick Pavlakis/Shutterstock Images, 13; Gianni Dagli Orti/Corbis, 18; Photos.com/Thinkstock,
23; Mikhail Markovskiy/Shutterstock Images, 24–25; Bettmann/Corbis, 28; World History Archive/
Alamy, 33; Christophe Boisvieux/Corbis, 35; VPC Travel Photo/Alamy, 36–37; Haris Vythoulkas/
Shutterstock Images, 41; North Carolina Museum of Art/Corbis, 45; Zoonar/N. Sorokin/Thinkstock,
46–47; Anthony Devlin/LOCOG/PA/AP Images, 48–49; DeAgostini/SuperStock, 51; Public Domain, 57;
Orestis Panagiotou/epa/Corbis, 60–61; Stefano Bianchetti/Corbis, 67; GraphicaArtis/Corbis, 68–69;
Ancient Art and Architecture Collection Ltd./Alamy, 75; Thanassis Stavrakis/AP Images, 77; Andrei
Ruchkin/Shutterstock Images, 78–79; Alamy, 83, 84; North Wind Picture Archives, 88; Erin Babnik/
Alamy, 90–91; Dorling Kindersley/Thinkstock, 94

Editor: Melissa York
Series Designer: Jake Nordby

Library of Congress Control Number: 2014943862

Cataloging-in-Publication Data

Bailey, Diane.
 Ancient Greece / Diane Bailey.
  p. cm. -- (Ancient civilizations)
ISBN 978-1-62403-538-8 (lib. bdg.)
Includes bibliographical references and index.
1. Greece--Civilization--To 146 B.C.--Juvenile literature. 2. Greece--History--Juvenile literature. 3.
Greece--Social life and customs--Juvenile literature. I. Title.
938--dc23

2014943862

CONTENTS

CHAPTER 1

A CROSSROADS OF CULTURES

One warm day approximately 2,500 years ago, the future Greek playwright Aeschylus had only one task: to tend the grapes, which were slowly ripening on the hillsides. It was not hard work, so it was no wonder Aeschylus fell asleep on the job. He had a dream, then, in which the god Dionysus—the one in charge of wine and festivals—visited him. The message Dionysus

Ruins of ancient Greek theaters still exist.

delivered to the teenaged Aeschylus in the dream was straightforward: become a playwright. Aeschylus began writing immediately. It took him years to perfect his craft, but eventually he went on to win many competitions at the Dionysia, a festival of theater that celebrated Dionysus. Aeschylus became a successful playwright and one of the most respected citizens of the Greek city-state Athens.

Aeschylus was at the height of his career in the early 400s BCE. At the time, Athens operated under a newly established democracy. This form of government that gave power to the masses would become widespread more than 2,000 years later. But in the first decades of the 400s BCE, democracy was controversial and still evolving. It was an idea, not an institution. Members of the aristocracy still struggled to retain power, and it was rarely a peaceful process.

On stage, Aeschylus's plays explored the conflict in real-life Athens and in other parts of Greece. In one of his plays, *The Eumenides*, Aeschylus seems to reveal his preferences for an aristocratic government. This view did not sit well with many of Athens's residents. At one point, Aeschylus was threatened while on stage. He also stood trial for revealing the secrets of the Eleusinian Mysteries, a religious cult based in his hometown. He was acquitted, but the political tide was against him. Shunned by his fellow citizens, Aeschylus moved to the island of Sicily, where he lived the rest of his life in peace.

In the middle of the 400s BCE, Greece was changing. The ancient mythology of gods and goddesses still dominated the culture, but an age of reason was emerging. Battles made heroes, and people celebrated military achievements, but Greeks were also developing more intellectual pursuits: math, science, theater, and philosophy. The political voices of the masses were coming together as they tried the new experiment of democracy. At this time, the city of Athens was at the heart of this crossroads in thinking. And ideas from this time in history still have resonance today.

OUT OF MYTHOLOGY

Ancient Greece was steeped in mythology. The Greeks believed Mount Olympus, in northern Greece, was home to a group of gods. Zeus hurled his thunderbolts when he was angry; Poseidon raised his trident to stir up storms on the sea; Apollo pulled the sun across the sky. In every way, the gods had control over people's lives. They could be temperamental, but they were not irrational. If people behaved well toward each other—and particularly if they

Mount Olympus

Located in northern Greece, Mount Olympus stands approximately 9,570 feet (2,920 m) at its highest point. The steep sides make it difficult to climb. The Greeks did not venture to the summit of Mount Olympus—that was the home of the gods, and they considered it off-limits to humans. In Greek mythology, it was a beautiful place, with never-ending nice weather, but at one time it had been a battleground, the place where Zeus led a campaign to overthrow his father Cronus, leader of the Titans. Zeus then became king of the gods and ruler on Mount Olympus.

treated the gods right—the gods would be appeased and allow people to live happy lives.

By as early as 700 BCE, the famous Greek poet Homer was composing his two masterpieces, the *Iliad* and the *Odyssey*. These epic poems are about the Trojan War and its aftermath. Many historians today believe the Trojan War did not actually happen—at least not in the way Homer describes it. But the story, which exalts the qualities of competition and military ability, inspired the Greek people for centuries. Much of ancient Greek history is a story of wars, as independent city-states fought to protect their borders.

CLASSICAL GREECE (450 BCE)

ATHENS★
SPARTA●
Mediterranean Sea

CRETE

N

Ancient Greece was not one but many places. Its physical borders were fragmented and far-flung, with colonies stretching from mainland Greece into what are now Italy, Bulgaria, Turkey, Iraq, Syria, and northern Africa. Greek civilizations sprang up on the thousands of islands sprinkled in the Mediterranean Sea and along most of the sea's shores. Greece was a people and a way of life more than it was a country.

As with other ancient civilizations, it is impossible to know the precise time "Greece" began. Tribes of people existed in the region for millennia, but the first substantial records begin in approximately 1400 BCE, with what is known as the Mycenaean civilization. This culture died by approximately 1100 BCE, and Greek history remains hazy until the Archaic Age (approximately 800–479 BCE). During this time, Greeks began leaving their homes in search of land to support the growing population. Fiercely proud and independent, they established numerous citizen-states, autonomous states in which the citizens ruled themselves. Eventually, the largest

The Blind Poet

Little is known about the Greek poet Homer, who lived in the 700s BCE. Some question whether Homer existed at all. Records say Homer was a blind, wandering poet, but this description is common in Greek legends, and the poet could also be a combination of several people. In any case, the stories attributed to Homer were likely not invented by him alone—they were the result of hundreds of years of an oral tradition of storytelling. Although today Homer's narratives are seen as mythical, the ancient Greeks believed the tales were their authentic history. Today, Homer's epic poems are considered a cornerstone of Western literature.

Stormy Seas

Living surrounded by water on the Greek peninsula and on many islands dotted across the Mediterranean and Black Seas, the Greeks naturally became a seafaring people. Still, choppy waters plagued sailors, and early ships weren't always seaworthy. The three-leveled triremes, used in war, were built for power, but water tended to leak in because shipwrights used lighter-weight wood prone to rot. Merchant ships, on the other hand, were sturdier but heavier and harder to navigate in coastal waters, where they could easily scrape against rocks. The Greeks developed a healthy caution for the water, particularly in the winter. The poet Hesiod of the 600s BCE warned, "Go to sea if you must, but only from mid-June to September, and even then you will be a fool."[1]

and most influential would be Athens. Although the story of Greece cannot be assigned to a single city, much of its known history comes from Athens, where the ideals that still influence Western society were born.

THE GOLDEN AGE

Aeschylus lived in what is now called the age of Classical Greece. It began, roughly, when the Greeks first experimented with democracy in approximately 510 BCE. For the next 150 to 200 years, Greece—and Athens in particular—made astonishing leaps forward in cultural development. Democracy was born, fought, rejected, revived, tweaked, and eventually celebrated. Pericles, a famous leader of Athens and a champion of democracy, began a public building campaign. Many examples still survive, most notably the spectacular Parthenon, a temple to the goddess Athena. Theater thrived, becoming a form of entertainment and political expression.

The Parthenon is one of the most famous ancient Greek buildings still standing.

Many of the great Greek philosophers who are remembered today lived during this time. Socrates asked probing questions of Athens's leaders and eventually died for his outspokenness. His student, Plato, wrote about the nature of the soul and the qualities of an ideal society. From Plato's way of thinking came Aristotle, who believed logic and reason should guide people's lives. Much of Western literature and philosophy today builds on elements found in the beliefs and writings of these ancient Greeks. The golden age of Classical Greece would launch a new era of government, art, drama, literature, and philosophy. But it had been a long time in the making.

CHAPTER 2

ON MEDITERRANEAN SHORES

wo civilizations dominate the early history of Greece. The Minoans lived primarily on the island of Crete, southeast of the Greek mainland. They thrived from approximately 2700 BCE to 1500 BCE, when evidence suggests earthquakes and volcanic eruptions might have destroyed the civilization.

The Minoan palace at Knossos has been partly restored.

The Minoans greatly influenced the Mycenaeans, who lived on the Greek mainland from 1400 to 1100 BCE. Both the Minoans and the Mycenaeans had sophisticated cultures. They built palaces with plumbing, painted elaborate pieces of art, and crafted exquisite gold cups and masks.

But after the Mycenaeans died out, Greece entered a dark age that lasted for centuries. The pieces of pottery that survive from this time show a much simpler style. Although farming certainly still existed, it was less complicated and there was more emphasis on animal herding than on growing crops. Nonetheless, the Greeks did not lose contact with the people around them, particularly in the Near East, including modern-day Turkey, Iraq, and Syria. Although written records were few and major milestones seemingly absent, the Greeks were building their knowledge base and forming beliefs and traditions that would provide the framework for later development.

RISE OF THE CITIZEN-STATES

By the 700s BCE, Greece was rebounding in what is now considered its Archaic Age. People adopted a new writing system for their language, and the first Olympic Games were held. The growing population put land at a premium. Mountains and rocky terrain made it difficult to grow crops, and arable land was scarce. Another problem was the Greek tradition of inheritance. Farms were divided equally among a man's sons. What began as a large farm was sliced up into smaller pieces with each generation unless the sons married women from wealthier families. Eventually, the small pieces weren't enough land to support a family.

To relieve the pressure and help their troubled economy, enterprising Greeks set out to find more land and establish colonies. New Greek settlements dotted the coasts around the Mediterranean Sea, from the mainland to the Peloponnese slightly to the south and west, as well as farther west across the Ionian sea in modern-day Italy, and east to Asia Minor in the current countries of Turkey and Syria. These new colonies, however, did not depend on their motherland. They were independent and self-ruling. The geography of Greece contributed to this system. Rugged mountains and valleys made travel difficult, and communication between communities was limited, if it existed at all. The people who settled on one side of a mountain were, more likely than not, isolated from the people who

Colonists or Exiles?

Many Greek colonists were eager to leave their homes in search of new land, but not all were so excited. In 706 BCE, Sparta had a group of men who were born outside of legal marriages who were becoming a problem. Although these people existed in other Greek cities as well, it was particularly a problem in Sparta because of the rigid social system. The men were were prohibited from becoming citizens and could not easily be a part of society. Their very existence caused unease within society. As a solution, Sparta decided to get rid of them, and it sent them to Taras, now Taranto, Italy. There, the men formed a new colony and a new life, but it was by force, not by choice.

The hoplite warrior was frequently represented in Greek art, including on vases.

lived on the other side. Thus, they were forced to be self-reliant, which nurtured a feeling of independence.

This led to the rise of the Greek citizen-state, or *polis*. Although it is commonly called a city-state, a polis was defined less by its geographic boundaries than by its people—the citizens—who counted themselves part of the city even if they lived outside the city itself. These hundreds of city-states, some tiny and some large, shared a common lifestyle and culture, but their governments were independent.

THE PERSIAN WAR

The ancient Greeks were under constant threat from Persia, a vast and powerful empire that lay to its east. The Persians wanted to bring the Greeks under their control, and resisting this effort became a central theme in Greek history, eventually helping to unite the diverse city-states. By the early 400s BCE, Darius, the king of Persia, began trying to conquer Greece to extend and strengthen the Persian Empire, located in modern Iran. On the surface it might have seemed a straightforward and relatively simple goal. The Persian armies were larger, stronger, richer, and better organized than the Greek soldiers. But perhaps Persia underestimated the Greeks' fighting spirit and strong sense of independence. When Persia attacked, they met hoplites. These Greek soldiers came from the middle class—they were neither aristocrats nor a professional army. They were interested in protecting their own land.

Although the smaller, weaker city-states gave in to some of Persia's demands, the larger ones resisted. According to one story, Persian representatives arrived in the city-state of Sparta and demanded earth and water as signs the Spartans recognized Persia's authority. The Spartans responded by tossing the Persians down a well, assuring them they would find plenty of earth and water at the bottom.

Nonetheless, Persia wasn't so easily rebuffed. In 490 BCE, approximately 25,000 Persian soldiers set sail across the Aegean Sea for Greece.[1] They landed at Marathon, a beach town north of the city of Athens. Although the Athenian force had fewer than one-half of the Persians' numbers, some shrewd military maneuvers allowed them to pull out a remarkable victory. The Persians were not discouraged, however. They regrouped and planned new attacks. Meanwhile, Athens built a navy and allied itself with Sparta, which also had a powerful military force.

When Persia attacked again in 480 BCE at Thermopylae, the Greeks were again severely outnumbered. But they managed to hold off the Persians, both at land and sea, until a traitor showed the Persian army a secret route to attack the Greeks. Sparta's King Leonidas, along with 299 members of his force, made a heroic last stand, fighting the Persians until every Spartan was killed—except for two who left before the battle. After the disaster at Thermopylae, the Athenian fleet met the Persians in

Marathon March

A hoplite force of approximately 10,000 Greek soldiers marched down to meet the Persian army at the beach at Marathon.[2] The Persians outnumbered them, but still the Greeks claimed a victory. The fleeing Persians were not retreating, however—they were on their way to Athens, which had been left unprotected when the Greek army went to the beach. The Greek general Miltiades now ordered his army back to Athens. Exhausted, bloodied, and weighted down with heavy armor, stories say they still made the 25-mile (40 km) march in only six hours and turned away the Persians once again. This event inspired the modern marathon.

the straits off the island of Salamis. This time the Greeks won, and the next year, in 479 BCE, the Greeks decisively defeated the Persians in a land battle at Plataea. This event is considered the start of the Classical Age.

THE STRUGGLE WITH SPARTA

After Persia was repelled, Athens's power grew. Democratic reforms spread and culture flourished. The city also established the Delian League, a group of allied Greek city-states, to continue defending itself against possible Persian attacks. The other Greek superpower, Sparta, continued to be Athens's ally, technically, but the relationship broke down through the 400s BCE. Athens, bolstered by a strong navy, seized more and more power. Open war broke out in 431, with Sparta arguing it was trying to free Greece from the iron fist of Athens.

For more than one-quarter of a century, the two powers struggled against one another, but eventually Athens lost. In 404 BCE, Sparta and her allies, the Peloponnesian League, finally captured the city of Athens, destroyed its navy, and forced it to surrender, ending the Peloponnesian War.

Some ancient Greeks believed Athens deserved its fate—that the city had used its political might unfairly. However, its power had strengthened much of Greece. Although Sparta emerged victorious from the Peloponnesian War, it was less effective as a governing force, and constant squabbling among the city-states left Greece, as a whole, weaker.

THE AGE OF ALEXANDER

With Athens and Sparta weakened, the Greek state of Macedon grew in power during the 300s BCE under the rule of King Philip II. When Philip's son Alexander, called "the Great," assumed the throne in 336 BCE, he wished to further increase the reach of Macedon and Greece. During his short reign, from 336 to 323 BCE, Alexander conquered lands south to Egypt and east into Asia, extending the Greek borders by some 3,000 miles (4,800 km).[3] He finally defeated the Persian Empire, which had threatened the Greeks for a long time.

Under Alexander, the Greek city-states lost much of their independence. He decided a network of separate entities, each with its own political agenda, was a threat to his absolute authority. Instead, he marched through Greece, bringing any people he encountered under his command—some by intimidation and others by force.

Alexander was a killing machine with little regard for those around him. He was also a brilliant general who achieved an astonishing amount during a short time. He stated that his mission was to free the Greeks, once and for all, from Persian control, and to unite the city-states under the banner of Panhellenism—a more homogenous Greek way of life. He did, indeed, achieve these goals, spreading the Greek empire thousands of miles. But becoming an empire brought changes. The center of cultural innovation shifted from the Greek mainland to new colonial cities, where purely Greek culture mixed with outside influences. Building upon the traditions of classical Greece, the new Hellenistic era began with Alexander's death and spawned its own art and ideas, including advances in science and technology.

Statues of Alexander the Great carved during his lifetime and shortly after still exist.

CHAPTER 3

CITIZENS AND SLAVES

The governments of classical Greece were as complex and varied as its many city-states. Some, such as early Athens, were ruled by oligarchies, composed of a few citizens from the elite classes. Because they concentrated power in the hands of just a few people, oligarchies were not always popular among those who were ruled. By the 600s BCE,

Citizens of ancient Athens met to do business and talk politics at the agora, where the Temple of Hephaestus still stands today.

rebellions and coups were common, and power was often seized by force by a single individual—a tyrant—who rallied support behind him. In the constantly changing landscape of power, Athens became a laboratory for government, and eventually it gave rise to a bold new form of government, called democracy.

THE AGE OF TYRANTS

In modern language, the word *tyrant* refers to a dictatorial, often cruel, leader. But in ancient Greece, a tyrant was simply someone who had seized power in a nontraditional way—that is, in a way other than inheriting it or being elected. In practical terms, this usually involved using force to overthrow the existing government. Tyranny in Greece, which reached its zenith from approximately 650 to 520 BCE, was a response to the Greek people rejecting the established oligarchies.

Although tyrants held their power alone, they were not necessarily evil or unfair. Many, but not all, were actually popular rulers. They often kept the social and economic structure in place so as not to disrupt daily living. They also typically passed their power down from father to son, though this rarely lasted longer than two or three generations. In this sense, tyranny was not so different from the rigid control of an aristocracy or oligarchy. However, it did represent a way of rejecting the old system, and it was an important step on the way to the rise of Greece's most famous, influential, and lasting legacy: democracy.

THE GRAND EXPERIMENT

By the 600s BCE, there was evidence of a more democratic government taking hold, particularly in Athens. A typical day at the agora—a central meeting place—would feature traders conducting business and men discussing politics. Members of the aristocracy became *archons*, the leaders who governed the city. All of Athens's male citizens were allowed to attend the Assembly, which elected the archons each year. This right was open to any citizen, rich or poor, although the archons still made all the decisions in the city's operation.

In approximately 621 BCE, the Athenians decided to write down the city's laws to prevent aristocrats from making thoughtless decisions. However, the Athenians' choice, Draco, made strict and merciless laws that were unfavorable to poor people. Athens was in an economic crisis, with more and more

Vote Them Out

Athenians devised a way to remove unpopular politicians, exiling them from the city. Each year, they could decide whether to hold an ostracism. Shards of broken pottery called *ostraka* were distributed to the Assembly members, and each could write the name of the man he wanted to see ousted. The person with the most unfavorable votes—a minimum of 6,000—was ostracized by being sent into exile for ten years.[1] Politicians who were thought to be pro-Persian or in favor of tyranny were often targeted.

money being concentrated in the hands of the rich. Conditions deteriorated rapidly as tensions rose between the haves and the have-nots. By the early 500s BCE, Athens found a new man to fix things. Solon was charged with trying to balance the demands of rich and poor, and he instituted several changes that promoted democracy. Among these were outlawing certain taxes and establishing several classes of citizens. These classes were based on wealth, rather than family heritage. Only the richest men could hold office. Although this doesn't seem democratic in modern times, it allowed people to work their way up the economic ladder to participate in politics.

In 508 to 507 BCE, another Athenian pushed the city even further down the path of democracy. Cleisthenes established a system that divided the population into ten tribes. Through voting, all male citizens could participate directly in making laws that governed the people, such as charging taxes, deciding how to spend the city's funds, and formulating military policy. In between Assembly meetings, a council of 500 men—50 from each of the 10 tribes—took care of day-to-day business.

Athens's practices still differed radically from those of a modern democracy. Neither women nor slaves were allowed to participate. Nor could *metics*—people who lived in Athens but were of foreign descent.

History and later artists have remembered Solon as a wise bringer of laws and organization.

Pericles

Pericles, a popular leader in Athens in the 400s BCE, was a staunch advocate of everything Athenian. "Our city is an education to Greece," he said in 431 BCE. "Future ages will wonder at us, as the present age wonders at us now."[3] He began the practice of paying men to perform jury service, which gave poorer citizens an opportunity to participate. On the other hand, he also sponsored a law that made it more difficult to become an Athenian citizen and thus enjoy the democratic privileges only given to citizens. He was hailed as a great democrat, but he did not hesitate to use his power. When playwrights poked fun at him, he banned their plays. The historian Thucydides wrote that with Pericles in power, Athens was "ostensibly a democracy but actually ruled by one man."[4]

These exclusions slashed the number of people with a voice in governance. Nevertheless, the democratic model in Athens vastly expanded the number of people who could participate in government from a few dozen to thousands. By the 450s BCE, democracy was well established.

SLAVES IN SOCIETY

The daily business of lawmaking in democracy takes a lot of time. One reason many ancient Greeks had the time to exercise this right was because there were other men and women who were not allowed to participate. Slaves were an integral part of Greek society and not just owned by rich families. Even middle-class families might have owned two or three slaves, whereas more affluent households might have had 15 or more.[2]

Aristotle justified the practice of slavery in his work *Politics*, writing "One that can foresee with his mind is naturally ruler and naturally master, and one that can do these things with his body is subject and naturally a slave. . . . The latter are strong for necessary service, the former erect and unserviceable for such occupations but serviceable for a life of citizenship."[5]

In many ways, a slave's life depended on where he or she lived. Different city-states had different standards for treating slaves. In Sparta, most slaves were treated harshly, and slaves in the silver mines outside of Athens worked long hours in horrific conditions. Inside the city of Athens, however, many slaves led comparatively easy lives. Household slaves were welcomed into the home with an official ceremony and often treated like family members. Slaves performed a variety of tasks. They tended crops and animals in the country and worked as artisans in the city. Even the city employed slaves to make arrests and run the prisons. Many slaves were paid. Records show male slaves earned approximately the same wages as free men for the

The Spartan Government

The city-state of Sparta had a combination government: its oligarchy of 28 men was headed by two kings who inherited power through their families. Spartan kings commanded the army. Occasionally the two disagreed on military strategy, hindering the army's effectiveness. Eventually the Spartans changed their policy so only one king was in charge at a time. The Spartan government also had a board of five overseers who had judicial powers and could keep the king in check if the need arose. The highly structured Spartan society prized personal responsibility and obedience, as evidenced by the proclamation issued by the overseers to the Spartan men: "Shave your mustache and obey the laws."[6]

same work, though most of their money went to their owners. With time, some slaves saved enough money to buy their freedom.

FARMERS AND TRADERS

Most surviving records from ancient Greece focus on the bustling city life and intellectual and political accomplishments of prominent citizens. However, for most Greeks, life did not revolve around philosophical questions or political ambitions. They were farmers, and they spent their days trying to support their households. The rugged terrain of Greece made farming challenging, but the region's access to water helped the Greeks establish trade with other civilizations on the Mediterranean and Black Seas. Metics probably found their niche in manufacturing and trade because they could not legally own land.

Mining was another important industry. The silver mines near Athens gave the city the financial means to build its navy and political might. Other silver and gold mines throughout Greece produced even more. Many of these came under the control of the kingdom of Macedon, helping fund its rise in power during the 300s BCE.

The political and economic structures of Greece were connected. Throughout history, Greeks had to fight to protect their land, both from outside threats and from other Greek people who sought to take it over.

Gold and silver mines allowed the ancient Greeks to produce beautiful treasures, such as this wreath of oak leaves and flowers from the 300s or 200s BCE.

Political and military decisions were made in order to promote economic growth, but struggles arose over who would benefit: aristocrats, or the ordinary people who produced goods? Whether life was easy or hard depended on where someone stood in the social order. Some changes were quick and dramatic, but most changes took centuries to occur.

A CLOSER LOOK

THE VIX KRATER

The ancient Greek historian Herodotus wrote in the 400s BCE of a bronze vessel so big it could hold hundreds of gallons of wine. He said the Spartans had made this jar, called a *krater*, for King Croesus of Lydia (in modern Turkey) in the middle of the 500s BCE. Modern historians dismissed Herodotus's claim. Certainly the Greeks used kraters to mix their wine, but they were small and meant to go on the dinner table.

Then, in 1953 CE, a French archaeologist excavating a grave found an enormous bronze vessel. Whether it is the same one Herodotus described isn't known, but the details matched. It is five feet (1.5 m) tall, weighs more than 450 pounds (500 kg), and has a capacity of 300 gallons (1,135 L).[7] The decoration on the vessel matches the Spartan style, though some modern historians disagree whether the Spartans manufactured it. Giant handles are shaped as fierce Gorgons, a mythical beast, and the drawings around the mouth of the jar show warriors marching into battle.

The jar is the largest discovered from the time, and it shows the Greeks had a lively trade far beyond their immediate area. The krater was found near the village of Vix, France, inside the grave of a Celtic princess. Twenty-five hundred years ago, this region was strategically located to control trade from current-day England down to Greece. Notably, tin from the mines was shipped south to be made into bronze. As products were shipped through the Vix region, the Celtic chieftains probably exacted a tax. Historians surmise that merchants offered the krater as a payment to the princess's family.

CHAPTER 4

DAILY LIFE

The fiercely independent Greek city-states were forever going to war and then making truces—until the next war. Despite their differences, however, the Greeks were united by their rich, established culture. They lived in a structured society in which daily life was predictable and rituals and customs dictated most behavior.

Men met to discuss philosophy and politics at parties called symposia, but citizen women were not allowed to attend.

37

MEN AND WOMEN

Greek society clearly defined the separate roles of men and women. Men had broader rights and freedoms than women. They were the only ones permitted to engage in political activity, and they handled anything associated with the military. They also assumed most of the financial responsibility for the family. Women contributed by taking care of most household tasks, such as cooking and weaving, either doing the work themselves or directing slaves. Poor women might work in the market.

Men and women usually socialized separately. Men hosted and attended symposia, parties at which there was food, drinks, and entertainment. Such events were closed to their wives and other respectable women, who were supposed to remain out of the public eye. In a play by Euripides, a character remarks, "There is one prime source of scandal for a woman—when she won't stay at home."[1] However, reality dictated that women leave the house at times. Particularly in the lower classes in which there were fewer slaves to do the work,

The Hetairai

Most women in Greek society lived restricted and somewhat secluded lives. They had nowhere near the same rights or freedoms enjoyed by men. A notable exception was with the hetairai. These women were paid to provide the entertainment at the symposia, and were known for their charm and engaging conversation skills. Often they could dance and play musical instruments, too. Hetairai usually came from a different city-state from where they worked and, unlike other women, they had the right to speak to men in public.

citizen women would go out to fetch water from public fountains or perform other chores. Tending the graves of family members was also the role of women, giving them another opportunity to mix with society. The city-state of Sparta offered somewhat of an exception to the rule. There, women enjoyed much more freedom. They could own property, and they wore much shorter skirts than in other parts of Greece. They were expected to keep physically fit and healthy so they could have strong children.

FROM BIRTH TO DEATH

Greek families wanted children—but not too many, because that diluted inheritances. To keep their numbers in check, the Greeks often subjected infants to harsh treatment. They stopped short of killing unwanted children, but girls and sickly babies might be put outside to let the gods decide their fate. Sometimes they died, but often they were rescued and brought up in another household. Once a child had been accepted into a family, it was treated well.

Some Greek children received a formal education, particularly those from wealthy families. Boys went to school beginning at age seven. They learned reading, writing, and math, and they studied music. Beginning at approximately age 12, boys took part in rigorous physical exercises to prepare them for military service, which they began at age 18. Girls did not attend formal schools but were taught by tutors at home. Spartan customs were somewhat different, and military service was the cornerstone of society. Boys were committed to military service from age seven to 30, and both boys and girls were expected to participate in physical activity.

Marriages were arranged early in children's lives, and usually mates were selected by the families to ensure the continuation of both families' fortunes. Girls were considered ready for marriage shortly after puberty, at age 14 or 15. Men, however, did not usually marry until they were close to age 30. There were few 50-year wedding anniversaries: the life expectancy for an ancient Greek was approximately 46 years old for men and 36 for women. Women often died in childbirth, which lowered the average. This was a relatively long life expectancy in the ancient world, probably aided by the Greeks' healthy diet and emphasis on exercise. At death, the women of the household prepared the body for burial, which occurred three days later, and then men and women came together for a feast.

FOOD, CLOTHING, AND SHELTER

Meeting the basic needs of food, clothing, and shelter took up much of the ancient Greeks' time and energy. Their diet consisted mostly of bread, as well as fruits and vegetables such as olives, asparagus, onions, cucumbers, cabbage, figs, and grapes. For protein, they ate fish, eggs, and cheese, as well as the meat from sheep and goats, often after the animals had been sacrificed to the gods, who were given their portion first. Wine was the preferred drink, but it was diluted with water to lessen the alcohol content.

Greek clothing was simple and practical. The peplos was a tunic, usually made of wool, fashioned into a rectangle that was draped over the shoulders and fastened with a pin. Loose armholes allowed freedom of movement. A chiton was a simple tunic crafted from a lighter-weight material such as linen.

The famous statues of the Acropolis wear the peplos style of dress.

Puppy Love

Dogs were an important part of Greek society. In mythology, the dog Cerberus stood guard at the entrance to the underworld, ruled by the god Hades. Dogs accompanied the goddess Artemis when she hunted. The Greeks also used dogs in their hunting, and the poet Homer notes that his hero, Odysseus, had a dog named Argos, which means "swift-footed." Most names corresponded to the qualities of speed, power, and physical appearance. The writer Xenophon, from the 400s BCE, wrote that short names were best and made a list of acceptable names. Common ones (translated) included Tracker, Butcher, Dagger, Stubborn, Happy, Jolly, Plucky, and, of course, the tried-and-true Whitey and Blackie.

Either garment could be brought in at the waist with a belt. Women's garments were floor-length, whereas men wore them at the knee. In colder weather, a cloak was worn over the tunic. Shoes were usually sandals or slippers, but there was no need for them inside the house, where everyone went barefoot.

Although few ruins of ancient Greek homes remain, scholars believe the styles were similar throughout the country. Examples from Athens show houses were typically built of dried mud and plaster with small windows. Most of them were rather flimsy and unimpressive. One writer from the time, Herakleides, remarked, "Most of the houses are mean, the pleasant ones few. A stranger would doubt, on first acquaintance, that this was really the renowned city of the Athenians."[2] Several rooms surrounded a central courtyard, and some houses had an upper floor. Often several generations of the family lived under one roof.

ART AND ARCHITECTURE

Much of what is known about Greek life comes from the remains of Greek art, mostly in the form of shards of pottery. In these scenes, people attend the theater or athletic competitions. Hoplites don their armor and go into battle—often accompanied by the Greek gods. Men at the symposia eat, drink, and listen to musicians. In the middle of the 400s BCE, scenes painted on vases expanded to show the activities of women—cooking, weaving, marrying, and taking care of children. Art styles and decorations changed gradually over the centuries, with scenes becoming more detailed and showing more emotional depth with time. Taken as a whole, they help reflect the ideas and values that defined Greek society.

The Greeks' busy trade with other civilizations affected their art greatly. In the 600s BCE, their contact with artisans on Crete and Cyprus influenced their work in metals, gems, and jewelry making. Bronze was a particularly popular material during the Archaic Age. It was

The Kindness of Strangers

If a stranger came knocking at the door, Greek custom dictated that it be opened and the person treated as a valued guest. The concept of xenia, meaning "hospitality," appears throughout Greek myths and stories. The god Zeus was the protector of travelers, and in one tale, he comes to Earth disguised as a mortal. He is refused a place to sleep several times before an old couple welcomes him. As punishment, he destroys the town but spares the people who took him in.

cheaper than gold or silver, but still durable, and it could be manipulated to produce a range of colors.

Unlike the unimpressive private homes, the public architecture in ancient Greece aimed to please the eye. It was solidly built of stone and marble. Columns formed the basic structural element. Three main types of columns can be traced to the ancient Greeks: Doric, Ionic, and Corinthian. Each had its own style and characteristics in terms of height, proportion, and type and amount of decoration, and each style dictated what the building as a whole would look like. A master architect oversaw the entire building project. He chose the stone, supervised the quarrying, and directed the craftsmen to cut it to size. Master carvers then added the final touches. Each stone fit so

Red and Black Pottery

Early Greek pots were made out of red clay and then decorated with figures etched in black. By the late 500s BCE, this style had been flip-flopped, with artists preferring red figures on a black background. Reversing the process gave artists more control in creating their figures. On black-figure pots, artists had to etch in details into the form, whereas in red-figure pottery, they could paint them with a brush. As a result, the scenes on red-figure pots are much more detailed and natural, better showing people's bodies, clothing, and facial expressions. Some artists also began signing their works, as a sense of pride of ownership emerged. Because sculptors were of higher status, it was more likely for them to sign their names than painters.

precisely in its place that the builders did not use mortar to fill the cracks. Metal clamps in the stones kept them from shifting in case of an earthquake.

Historians have learned much about ancient Greece from its vases.

45

A CLOSER LOOK

BUILDING THE PARTHENON

The Parthenon is one of the most famous structures in the world, the ultimate monument to ancient Greece. It has stood for almost 2,500 years. In the 400s BCE, under the leadership of Pericles, the Athenians undertook a huge public building project. The centerpiece was the Parthenon, a massive temple to Athens' patron goddess, Athena. The spectacular building was completed in a little more than a decade.

To build it, the Greeks removed thousands of tons of marble from a quarry approximately 11 miles (18 km) from Athens. They hewed it into blocks, then brought the blocks back to the city. They had to haul the heavy blocks to the top of the Acropolis, a flat, raised plateau of rock at the heart of the city. There, they painstakingly fit the blocks together, using iron clamps to secure them.

Next came the detail work: artisans carved delicate grooves down the sides of each of the Parthenon's columns—46 around the perimeter and 39 more inside. After that, they applied a final rough texturing, chiseling the marble with thousands of tiny nicks to cover any imperfections in the stone. Finally, they painted it. Although the remains of the Parthenon today are gray, it was originally colored in striking hues of blue, green, and red.

Current restorations of the Parthenon are taking much longer than the original construction. For one thing, modern architects think the ancient Greeks had some technological advantages compared with today's methods, such as specialized tools that let them cut and carve faster. Even so, restoration is painstaking work. The Parthenon has been heavily damaged over the years, with pieces strewn all over the site. This means restorers have had to figure out where everything fits even before they can start putting it together again. They're also trying to add as little new material as possible. Previous attempts at restoration actually harmed the structure, so now restorers are taking the time to do it right.

CHAPTER 5

IDEAS AND IDEALS

Perhaps more than anything else, the Greeks are remembered for their deep thinking about life and the world. Whereas philosophers spoke of harmony and self-awareness, ordinary people prized physical fitness and competitiveness. Together, these ideals played out in the rituals and traditions that defined regular Greek life.

The modern Olympic Games pay homage to the ancient ones with a torch lighting ceremony at the site of the ancient event.

THE OLYMPIC GAMES

Festivals and religious ceremonies regulated the days, seasons, and years of the ancient Greeks. No event was bigger than the Olympic Games, which were held every four years. The date for the first Olympic Games is officially 776 BCE, but they probably dated to an even earlier time in the form of a festival held to honor Zeus. The first games featured only one event, a sprint, but they expanded quickly. By the 500s BCE, the games included chariot races, long jumping, and discus and javelin throwing. Boxing, wrestling, and overall fighting were combined in a particularly grueling event called the pankration, which had few rules. Competitors were banned from biting their opponent or trying to gouge out his eyes during the pankration, but kicking and choking were perfectly acceptable.

No foreigner athletes were eligible to participate, and because of the time needed to train and compete, competitors usually came from the ranks of the aristocracy. Women were not allowed to compete. Married women could not even attend the games because it was considered improper, although single women could.

Winners at the games did not receive any money as a prize. Instead, they were awarded a wreath woven from wild olive branches. A victor might also be honored with a feast, and sometimes a poem or statue was commissioned

Charioteer, 550–530 BCE, black-figure pottery vase

to commemorate his victory. The poet Pindar wrote about one winner, "When they saw you many times victorious . . . each of the maidens was speechless as they prayed you might be her husband or son."[1] Not all agreed with celebrating the victors, however. The philosopher Xenophanes argued, "It isn't right to judge strength as better than good wisdom."[2]

Nevertheless, a primary function of the games was to encourage physical excellence. Men who showed strength and endurance proved worthy of serving in the military. Athletes competed naked, which fit the Greek ideal of promoting physical fitness and attractiveness. The competition focused on individual rather than team events. Who was fastest? Who was strongest?

Aiming to be the best dovetailed with the Greeks' competitive spirit and their emphasis on being able to subdue an enemy.

As with other rituals, the games also had a religious aspect, and sacrifices were held beforehand. Athletes consulted the gods for guidance in the competition, but there were no guarantees, and defeat for some was unavoidable. The intense spirit of competition in the Greek world meant a loss could be shameful and humiliating.

THE DRAMATIC APPROACH

The tradition of theater in Greek life was also rooted in religion. In Athens, an annual theater festival called Dionysia celebrated the Greek god who

The First Historians

The historian Herodotus of the 400s BCE spent his life roaming through Greece, asking questions and collecting stories along the way. Eventually he wrote his masterpiece, *The Histories*, an account of the Greco-Persian wars from 499–479 BCE. He is sometimes called the father of history. Although his work was comprehensive, it was also full of fantastical anecdotes. Thucydides, another historian who wrote approximately a generation after Herodotus, took a just-the-facts approach, and he questioned the accuracy of Herodotus's accounts. But Herodotus never let the truth slow him down. He even included a disclaimer to readers in *The Histories*, writing, "I am obliged to record the things I am told, but I am certainly not required to believe them."[3]

oversaw wine and entertainment. Central to the festival was the spirit of competitiveness. Each year, the city's leading playwrights would submit a trilogy of tragic plays, plus a lighthearted play that provided comic relief.

The competition was fierce but fair. The rules stated that all plays had the same number of cast members: three actors to play the leading roles plus 15 chorus members. There was a drawing to decide which of the best actors would perform in which of the competing plays, so as not to give anyone an unfair advantage. Male actors played all the parts, even the women characters. The winning playwrights earned a special respect among the Athenians. It wasn't only the writers who wanted recognition, though. The wealthy citizens of Athens built prestige by financing the productions, which required more than 1,200 actors and singers all together.[4]

Most of the Greek tragedies focused on the interplay between men and the gods. Comedies, on the other hand, might look frankly at more everyday

Acting Out

Theatrical productions became more elaborate as time went on, with more scenery, more sophisticated costumes, and even special effects. For example, a crane was used to lift actors and fly them across the stage to mimic the gods. When the playwright Aeschylus began working in the mid-400s BCE, most plays had only one actor and a chorus, a group of background observers who commented on the action. Aeschylus introduced the idea of a second actor to heighten the drama while reducing the role of the chorus. He also had actors wear elaborate costumes, masks, and platform shoes so the audience could see them better.

matters. Aristophanes's comedies offer an intimate look into the more seedy aspects of Athenian life. Plays explored political and cultural issues facing the Greeks and offered a way to bring new ideas and opinions to the thousands of people watching.

THE GREEK PHILOSOPHERS

"What do *you* think?" A student of Socrates, one of ancient Greece's most important philosophers, would have heard that question many times. Socrates didn't tell his students what to believe. Instead, he asked questions until they arrived at their own conclusions. Socrates went against the traditional ways of Athenian society in the 400s BCE. Rather than pursue

Learning the ABCs

The Mycenaean society used a form of writing called Linear B, which consisted of approximately 90 syllables that were combined to form words. By approximately 800 BCE, the Greeks had adopted a different system. They were in contact with the Phoenicians, who used an alphabet that was all consonants. The letters were strung together, and the reader or speaker had to remember which vowels went where. The Greeks took this language and made some modifications. The Phoenicians used some consonants the Greeks did not, so they borrowed those unneeded symbols and assigned them vowel sounds. Now any word could be written down. The new alphabet helped literacy spread through Greece, and the Greek system became the basis for other alphabets, including the one used in English.

power and fame, he instead questioned the greater rights and wrongs of society, often speaking up for the underdog when no one else did. Socrates worked to broaden the role of philosophy. Making sense of the physical world wasn't enough. Rather, he encouraged men to understand their inner thoughts and value systems.

Although Socrates recorded none of his beliefs in writing, he is remembered through the records of his students, notably Plato, who lived from 428 to 348 BCE. Plato built on the ideas of Socrates and added his own. He wrote in the form of dialogues, with Socrates regularly appearing as a character. Plato was passionate about examining the ideals of society and how they succeeded or failed in real life. In the *Republic*, he wrote about a society that was governed by a wise king and not tainted by the greed or passions of ordinary people.

Similar to his teacher Socrates, Plato explored the idea that people go through life without realizing their intellectual limitations because they have known nothing else. Plato explained this in his story

The Trial of Socrates

In 399 BCE, Socrates faced criminal charges. His offenses, according to the court, were corrupting the youth and showing impiety, meaning he would not recognize the gods the city recognized. The accusations were likely motivated by politics. Socrates criticized some aspects of democracy, which threatened the democratic leadership that was struggling to survive. Socrates was found guilty by a jury of 500 men, with a vote of 280 to 220.[5] Socrates maintained his innocence, and his defiant attitude angered the jury, which sentenced him to drink poisonous hemlock to bring on his death.

"The Cave." In this story, men live in a cave, watching shadows of people and animals move on the wall. This is all there is to their life, until one man leaves the cave. He realizes the shadows are only representations of real objects, and life is infinitely more complex than he previously realized.

Plato's most famous student was Aristotle, who studied with him for 20 years. Aristotle, who lived from 384 to 322 BCE, was fascinated with marine biology and physics, and his philosophical realizations often came from what could be observed and measured in the physical world. He was interested in developing ways of thinking that reflected the reality of the natural world. Aristotle's contributions were a unique combination of the scientific and the philosophical. The way he brought the two together reflects his importance as a founder of the scientific tradition, one of Greece's most important legacies.

Famous Italian painter Raphael created the *School of Athens* in 1510. Plato and Aristotle stand together under the arch at the center.

A CLOSER LOOK

AT THE AGORA

Key:

1. Law Court
2. Mint
3. Enneakrounos (fountainhouse)
4. South Stoa I and South Stoa II (a stoa is a columned porch or arcade with shops and offices)
5. Law Court
6. Strategeion (political meeting room)
7. Colonos Agoraios (meeting place for craftsmen)
8. Tholos (eating and living space for politicians)
9. Agora boundary marker
10. Monument of the Eponymous Heroes (a statue where announcements were posted)
11. Metroon (Old Bouleuterion) (temple)
12. New Bouleuterion (political meeting room)
13. Temple of Hephaestus
14. Temple of Apollo Patroos
15. Stoa of Zeus
16. Altar of the Twelve Gods (temple)
17. Stoa Basileios (Royal Stoa)
18. Temple of Aphrodite Urania
19. Stoa of Hermes
20. Stoa Poikile

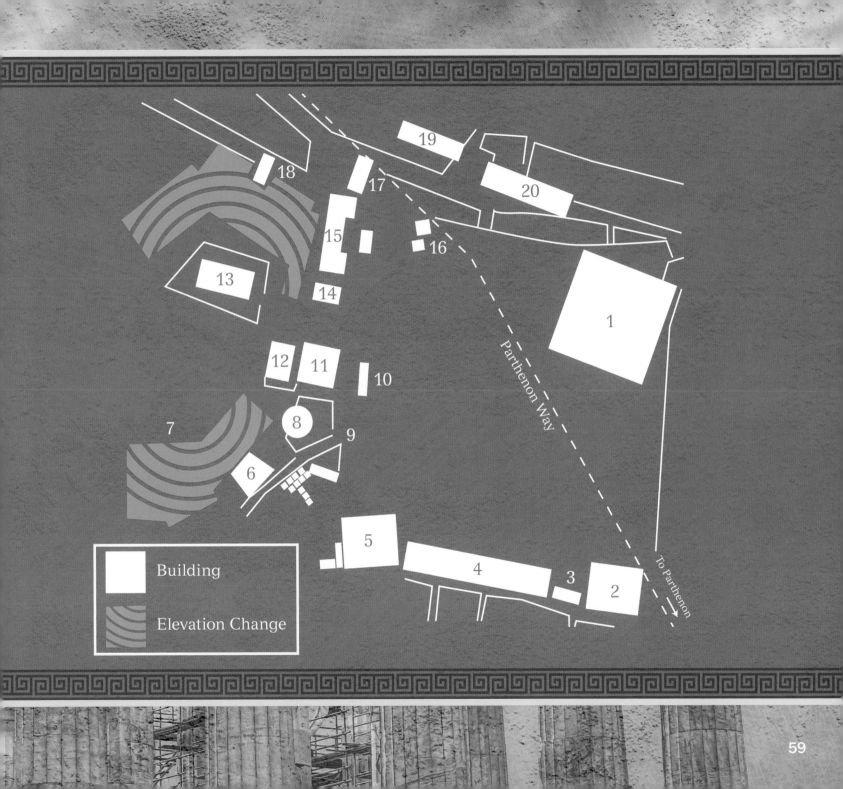

Building

Elevation Change

Parthenon Way

To Parthenon

CHAPTER 6

IN SERVICE TO THE GODS

As is typical in the religion of many cultures, the Greek myths served to explain how the world began and how humans developed. The gods controlled everything, but they could be fickle beings. Sometimes they were helpful, but just as often they were mischievous and meddlesome. Either way, their actions trickled down to affect humans.

Many surviving works of art from ancient Greece depict the gods, including this statue of the god Poseidon in the Archaeological Museum of Athens.

A PANTHEON OF GODS

The Greeks were pantheistic, meaning they believed in many gods. In the Greek community of gods, each had certain powers and weaknesses, a realm of life over which they were in charge, and a distinct personality. The Greek gods resembled humans in many ways, from their physical appearance to their personalities. The most important gods, the Twelve Olympians, had power over most things, but there was an assembly of lesser gods as well.

At the top of Mount Olympus was Zeus. Although he might delegate power to his wife, Hera, and his several children, in the end his word was law. Hera was in charge of married women, even though she had trouble in

The Nichoria Bone

A million years ago, giant mammals roamed the Mediterranean. The ancient Greeks later discovered some of their bones. One, the Nichoria Bone, has now been identified as the thigh bone of a woolly rhinoceros. Modern archaeologists found it in the early 1970s CE at the Nichoria Acropolis, a sanctuary in the Peloponnese region of Greece, where it had been put on display. Scientists determined the early discoverers had transported it from the Megalopolis Basin, a site 35 miles (56 km) away. Adrienne Mayor, a researcher from Stanford University, points out that its original location coincides with the place the ancient Greeks called the "Battleground of the Giants." She believes the great beasts in Greek mythology may have been an attempt to explain the origins of the bones.

her own marriage with Zeus. He was always with other women, so Hera was always devising ways to punish them. Zeus's brother Poseidon ruled the seas, and his other brother Hades was in charge of the underworld and the dead. Zeus's daughter and favorite child was Athena, a powerful goddess in charge of civilization, crafts, and agriculture. Apollo, Zeus's son, was the god of the sun, revered for beauty and truth. Apollo's twin sister, Artemis, reigned over Earth and nature. Aphrodite, another daughter of Zeus, was the goddess of love and beauty, and his son Hermes, who was swift and shrewd, kept watch over commerce and trade. The god of war, Ares, was the least-favorite son of Zeus and Hera: the poet Homer reports that both his parents despised him. Rounding out the dozen were Hephaestus, the god of fire, and Hestia, the protector of the home.

CRIME AND PUNISHMENT

Humans needed the gods' help at times. They made offerings and sacrifices to ensure a good harvest or the health of a child. Much of the year was taken up with numerous holidays and festivals that revolved around recognizing the gods' superiority and power. Humans tried to channel this power to their benefit—or at least ward off the gods' revenge. In Greek mythology, one theme came up again and again: it didn't pay to anger the gods. A powerful example was the story of Prometheus.

Getting Revenge

Sometimes the Greeks might enlist the help of the gods to inflict harm on people who had wronged them. They wrote a curse on a thin lead tablet, describing the punishment they desired and the name of their enemy—perhaps a political rival, a thief, or even a spouse. Then they heated and rolled up the lead sheet to hide the writing, often tucking in herbs or some of the intended victim's hair for added potency. Then they tossed it into a pit at a sanctuary or a fresh grave. There the curse tablet could make its way to the gods, who could decide whether to carry out the curse.

Prometheus was himself a god, but he was not as strong as the all-powerful Zeus. One time, Prometheus tricked Zeus. Prometheus let Zeus choose between two offerings of a calf. One was of good quality but disguised to look poor, whereas the other was of poor quality but dressed up to be attractive. Zeus chose the better-looking one. This meant humans would henceforth keep the meat of their sacrifices and give the gods the skin and bones. Zeus was angry, so he withheld fire from humans to make their lives harder. Once again, however, Prometheus outwitted the great god. He stole fire by hiding it in the stalk of a fennel plant. Then he smuggled it to Earth and gave it to humans. Now Zeus was furious. This time he exacted a worse revenge. He chained Prometheus to a stake and sent an eagle to eat out his liver. At the end of the day, Prometheus—being immortal—would heal and be subjected to the same punishment the next day. Zeus's half-human son Herakles eventually freed Prometheus. But Zeus wasn't finished with humans. At the time, all humans were men. Zeus asked the goddesses to create a woman, Pandora, and sent her to Earth, where she made trouble for men.

HEROES OF OLD

In addition to the immortals, Greek mythology features numerous examples of heroes and heroines who interacted with the gods on behalf of humans. Heroes were semidivine beings, often the offspring of a god and a mortal. This let them feel more sympathy for humans than the fully immortal gods. But heroes had a connection to the world of immortals that humans could never attain. Heroes and heroines could cross back and forth, giving people a glimpse, and perhaps an understanding, of a larger existence and purpose.

Theseus, legendary founder of the city of Athens, traveled to the ancient kingdom of Minos and killed the Minotaur, the half-man, half-bull beast that regularly devoured unlucky young Athenians sent as sacrifices. Strong and shrewd, the half-god hero Herakles redeemed his wrongdoings by embarking on the most difficult challenges the gods could devise, slaying monsters and stealing precious items. Perseus was another beast-killing hero, and he became the legendary founder of the civilization of Mycenae.

ASKING THE ORACLE

The Greeks used other methods to communicate with the gods. Oracles were priestesses who could supposedly receive messages from the gods and then convey them to mortals. One of the most famous oracles was in Delphi, at a temple to Apollo. At Delphi, Apollo spoke through his priestesses, who relayed his messages to those who had made the steep climb up the mountain, gave a rich gift, and offered an appropriate sacrifice. Anyone could consult the oracle, not just Greeks, but Greeks got first priority.

Humans consulted oracles with a variety of questions, from how an athlete would perform at the Olympic Games to which army was likely to be favored in battle. Should two people get married? Should they farm? Where should a new colony be established? The answers were usually vague and sounded like riddles. They could be—and typically were—interpreted in different ways, depending on what the asker wanted to happen.

Seers also had a role in helping humans navigate the mysterious world of the gods. Seers didn't relay the gods' messages as oracles did. Instead, they interpreted what were believed to be signs from the gods. These signs were not always obvious— the gods might disguise their messages in the

Mysterious Ways

A sacred place for Greeks was at Eleusis, which was home to a sophisticated cult for Demeter, the goddess of the harvest. Each September, to celebrate the cycle of death and rebirth, members went through an elaborate process involving purifying baths, sacrifices, and dances. These rites, known as the Eleusinian Mysteries, were kept a secret from anyone not in the cult, upon threat of death. The cult remained popular for hundreds of years until the Christian emperor Theodosius shut it down in the 300s CE.

A later artist imagines what it would have been like to visit the oracle at Delphi.

organs and entrails of sacrificed animals, for example. Seers were educated, respected, and usually well paid for their services, which included offering advice on political and military matters.

The Greeks diligently tried to communicate with, and often appease, the gods. However, with time they recognized many things were governed by the laws of nature, not the gods. It fell to early Greek scientists to begin offering rational explanations to life's mysteries.

HAVEN OF THE BLESSED
PRIME MOVER OF THE SPHERES
LIBRATION
LIBRATION
SPHERE OF FIXED STARS
SPHERE OF ♄ SATURN
SPHERE OF ♃ JUPITER
SPHERE OF ♂ MARS
SPHERE OF ☉ THE SUN
SPHERE OF ♀ VENUS
SPHERE OF ☿ MERCURY
SPHERE OF ☽ THE MOON
FIRE
AIR
EARTH
WATER

CHAPTER 7

THE FIRST SCIENTISTS

I n 585 BCE, a battle was raging between the civilizations of Lydia and Media, in Asia Minor (modern-day Turkey). All of a sudden, the sky darkened. The soldiers looked up, confused and awed, as something moved in front of the sun and blotted it out. How could the sun vanish in the middle of the day? The two sides took the event as a bad omen, a message

The ancient Greeks were great astronomers, tracking several planets they believed moved in separate spheres around Earth.

that the gods disapproved of their fighting. To appease the gods, they quickly reached a peace agreement. What they had actually witnessed was a solar eclipse. According to legend, one man had known it was coming. He was Thales of the city Miletus, a place that experienced a revolution of thought in the 600s and 500s BCE.

EXAMINING THE WORLD

Miletus was located in eastern Greece, in a region called Ionia in current-day Turkey. Trade, colonization, and war brought the people in frequent contact with civilizations in the areas of modern-day Egypt and Iraq. They exchanged goods and also ideas, customs, and styles. Poetry flourished and parties became a popular form of socializing and entertainment. Philosophy and science also thrived as leading thinkers asked questions and pushed the boundaries of what was known and believed. This period during the 500s and 600s BCE, called the Ionian Enlightenment, would influence the remarkable achievements of scientists during the golden age of classical Greece.

Thales, the most famous and influential philosopher of the time, was also a scientist. Stories say he predicted the solar eclipse that so startled the warring soldiers. He may have done so by observing the timing between lunar and solar eclipses so he could calculate when it was coming. Whatever his methods, it helped establish Thales as one of history's first scientists.

Thales was not only known for his study of astronomy; he also theorized that everything came from water and that Earth floated on it. Two of his students, Anaximander and Anaximenes, questioned and built on Thales's theories, arguing that perhaps everything in fact came from air or from another unknown substance. A century and a half later, during the heyday of classical Greece, the innovative thinker Democritus devised another theory: that all matter was composed of tiny particles called atoms. Although Democritus was wrong about a few things—for example, he believed all atoms were made of the same material and only differed in shape and size—his explanation was remarkably advanced for his time.

Although modern knowledge goes far beyond what Thales studied and disproves some of it, he is hailed for establishing a scientific process that still is followed today. He attempted to answer questions

Hippocrates

Hippocrates of Cos, an early figure in Greek medicine, wrote several papers with his followers examining different medical conditions in the 400s and 300s BCE. These were primarily case studies that took a logical approach to medicine. One paper looks at the disease of epilepsy. Hippocratic doctors argued against calling it a disease from the gods simply because its true causes were not understood. Instead, in the Hippocratic tradition, doctors emphasized observation and treating the body as a whole organism. Echoes of Hippocrates are still found in the Hippocratic Oath, taken by many doctors when they enter the medical profession. In it, doctors pledge to use their knowledge only for good and never for harm.

about the natural world with rational explanations, rather than attribute phenomena to the actions of the gods. The processes of observation and collecting evidence took hold with Thales, as did the practice of questioning scientific theories in a professional manner by supporting or contradicting them with new evidence.

PIONEERS IN MATH

Although the Greeks certainly didn't invent or discover mathematics, they were among the first to study it as an actual discipline. They grasped the concepts and abstractions of math, whereas previous civilizations had only applied it in practical situations. The Greeks studied the ideas of irrational numbers, prime numbers, and infinity.

The famous Pythagorean theory states that in a right triangle—one with a 90-degree angle—the squares of the two shorter sides added together will equal the square of the longest side, the hypotenuse. The Greek Pythagoras, who receives credit for this theory, was not actually the first to notice it. The Chinese had noticed the relationship centuries before. But Pythagoras, who lived in the 500s BCE, pointed out that the formula didn't just work occasionally. It applied *every* time, without exception. What's more, he proved it. It was that part that made Pythagoras's theory so significant. The concept of the mathematical proof gave structure and stability to the study of math. It was one of the greatest contributions to the field.

Every thorough education in math includes geometry, but it might not have been that way without the Greeks, particularly Euclid, who lived in the 200s BCE. Euclid did not invent geometry; it had been studied long before he lived. Although he did not unearth new mathematic principles, he explained the ones that were known in an organized way so that a learner could logically build his or her knowledge. His primary work, *The Elements*, doesn't just cover geometry, however. It consists of several volumes and also covers algebra and number theory. It was designed to be an introduction to mathematics, and it remained an essential textbook for centuries after it was written.

ENGINEERING AND TECHNOLOGY

The Greeks were good at using simple tools such as drills, hammers, saws, and chisels. Lifting massive blocks of stones to build the temples to the gods

Harmony in Numbers

Pythagoras noticed many similarities between math and music. Fascinated by both, he showed how musical scales adhere to certain mathematical ratios. For example, a string plucked on a guitar will make a certain note. If the length of the string is halved, such as by pressing it against a fret board, the note sounded will be one octave higher. Pythagoras even believed people were like musical instruments. They had to be tuned to be in harmony with the rest of the world.

or loading cargo from ships were heavy tasks. Ancient records describe how the Greeks invented complex systems of pulleys and levers to perform monumental tasks. They experimented with the physics of flight and built what is considered the first mechanical computer, which was designed to make astronomical predictions.

They also showed skill in metalworking, exhibited in items from enormous bronze vessels to exquisite jewelry, and they learned to control the use of heat in forging different metals. They had rudimentary plumbing and built tunnels and aqueducts to deliver water to cities.

Legend says the mathematician Archimedes (290–212 BCE) ran naked through the streets after a profound moment of discovery. He had been taking a bath and suddenly realized the volume of his body could be measured by the amount of water he displaced. The story of his impulsive action might be false, but Archimedes did make great strides in learning how to calculate weight, area, and volume using water displacement.

Mapping It Out

The Greek Anaximander, who lived in the 500s BCE, is credited for producing the first map of the world, beginning the Greeks' entry into cartography. Anaximander envisioned Earth as a short, wide cylinder, similar to a hockey puck. Three land masses—Europe, Asia, and Libya—rested on the top, arranged around the Mediterranean and Black Seas at the center. The ocean surrounded the perimeter. Anaximander also created a globe that showed the relationship of Earth to other celestial bodies. However, in his version, Earth and the sun were the same size, and the stars were closer to Earth than either the sun or the moon.

The Archimedes screw was used to move water up hills.

He also described the mathematics of using levers to lift heavy objects. The invention of the simple screw, a basic machine now used in countless applications, is credited to Archimedes. The methods used by the Greeks— and the fact that they wrote down *how* they did things—helped lay the foundation for a world dependent on technology.

A CLOSER LOOK

THE ANTIKYTHERA MECHANISM

In 1901, divers investigating an ancient shipwreck in the waters off Greece found an amazing artifact which has since been described as the world's first analog, or mechanical, computer. The Antikythera Mechanism, dated to the 100s BCE, is a sophisticated mass of bronze gears that looks somewhat like a complex alarm clock. Rather than waking the ancients up in time for work, however, researchers have determined the device functioned as an astronomical calendar. More than 30 gears, housed inside a wooden box, worked together to show the positions of the sun, moon, and the five planets the ancient Greeks knew about.

Modern researchers used X ray technology to find tiny inscriptions on the device that indicate its purpose. They found words such as "Venus," "little golden sphere" (probably the sun), and "stationary" (perhaps noting how planets seem to stop moving at times). By turning a dial, a person could choose a certain date. Gears connected to the main dial then rotated to show where celestial bodies were located on that date. Earth does not orbit the sun in a perfect circle; it travels more in an ellipse, or elongated circle.

The device's creators changed the spacing on the device to account for this irregular pattern.

Much expense and craftsmanship went into creating the device. Scholars believe it was probably a luxury item because it would have been easier and cheaper to calculate the astronomical cycles by hand.

CHAPTER 8

MILITARY MUSCLE

From the fearsome sight of a red-cloaked Spartan army to the sleek profile of an Athenian warship, the evidence of war was everywhere in ancient Greece. War was a necessary undertaking in the constant effort to preserve the Greeks' lifestyle. Greece was tiny in comparison with the vast Persian Empire, which frequently threatened to overtake the smaller

Warriors were frequently represented in ancient Greek art.

civilization. In addition, the Greeks were constantly proving themselves to each other through war—it was part of the fabric of their being. Plato called war "Always existing by nature between every Greek city-state."[1] Battles might be won or lost, but they were rarely avoided.

THE HOPLITES

The warfare the poet Homer described in his famous poems was largely an undertaking of the aristocracy, with a focus on a few elite individuals. Even in early Greek fighting there were massed battles involving ordinary soldiers, but these battles did not receive much attention. By the 600s BCE, this emphasis was changing. Greece was rebounding from its Dark Age, stabilizing its social and economic systems, and colonizing new areas. More land was distributed among the middle class rather than being concentrated in the hands of the aristocracy. However, this land was often located in inhospitable terrain, making its borders difficult to access or navigate. As a result, the primary responsibilities of defense and protection fell to the people who were on site: the owners of the land. As it did, a new style of warfare emerged with the hoplite.

A hoplite was a citizen-soldier. He was concerned with establishing his political and economic position in the community and then defending that position when the need arose. Hoplites had an economic advantage in that they owned land—which provided them with money—and in return they paid for their own equipment. They came primarily from the middle class, since most members of the lower classes could not afford to buy their own arms and armor. Brisk trade with neighboring civilizations also hastened the rise of hoplite warfare, as it gave the Greeks access to metal for strong weapons and armor. Many historians believe the emergence of the hoplite led to the spread of political power to the middle classes. These men risked death as they fought for their land while paying for their own defense. They would naturally feel entitled to greater influence in how things were run.

The physical formation of an army of hoplites was a phalanx, a large rectangle in which soldiers stood next to one another in tightly packed rows. They were burdened under the weight of heavy metal armor, spears, and shields, their vision and hearing hindered by claustrophobic helmets.

A CLOSER LOOK

HOPLITE ARMOR

Ancient Greek soldiers were armed with swords and spears and used heavy bronze armor to protect themselves. Armor called a cuirass covered the torso. Leg armor called greaves fitted over the calves and was sculpted to resemble the leg muscles. Early helmets were bell shaped, covering the skull but leaving the face unprotected. Later ones evolved to cover most of the head and face, with ear and nose plates and narrow slits at the eyes. Some were elaborately decorated, with serpents twisting above the eyes, lions on the cheek pieces, and ruffles of horsehair on the top to form a crest.

Such sturdy armor came with some drawbacks. The armor was hot and heavy, making it uncomfortable and difficult to move around. The helmets restricted the soldiers' ability to see and hear. Still, many historians believe the phalanx formation helped to protect the soldiers. Most were stationed in the interior of the phalanx so their fellow soldiers offered a physical barrier from the enemy. Their shields offered another line of defense. When the men were lined up in the phalanx, 3 feet (1 m) apart, the shields overlapped to form a protective wall.

Trireme rowers sat on three levels so the ships could fit more oars for a faster trip.

Consequently, the hoplite style of fighting was a brutal clash of metal, as opposed to nimble fighting. Archilochus, a poet from the 600s BCE, described the ideal hoplite as "a short man firmly placed upon his legs, with a courageous heart, not to be uprooted from the spot where he plants his feet."[2]

WAR ON THE WATER

The Greek city-states were scattered on islands and coasts, and battles inevitably happened at sea. Warships were powered by rowing, and for a long time, the most efficient design was a penteconter, a ship that carried 50 oarsmen seated on a single level. Eventually this evolved into a two-level ship that could hold more men. By approximately 700 BCE, the Greeks had developed the trireme. This three-level ship fit 160 to 170 oarsmen, plus additional soldiers and officers, for a total of approximately 200 men. Ramming enemy ships was the primary form of battle, and the triremes, with their additional manpower, were ideal for this maneuver. Triremes had drawbacks, however. They sank easily, and they couldn't stay at sea for long because they could not carry enough supplies to feed the crew.

Nonetheless, the trireme came to define the Athenian navy. In 483 BCE, the military general and politician Themistocles went to the Athenian archons and proposed a radical idea: build ships— a lot of them. Athens had just discovered a deposit

All Boarded Up

The priestess at the Oracle at Delphi was always difficult to interpret. When the Athenians asked for her prediction on the war with Persia in 480 BCE, the reply was that "wooden walls" would save the Greeks.[3] This prompted a flurry of speculation. Some believed the oracle referred to the walls around the Acropolis. But the military general Themistocles interpreted the wooden walls to be the ships of Athens's navy. The navy did indeed defeat the Persians at the Battle of Salamis, while those who had chosen to barricade themselves behind a wooden wall in Athens were killed.

of silver in nearby mines. Themistocles suggested using the windfall to build 200 triremes. The archons agreed, and within three years Athens had produced the ships for a powerful navy. Themistocles's timing was good: the new naval force proved critical when the Greeks faced the Persians at Salamis in 479 BCE.

THE SPARTAN STYLE

Although the Athenians were the undisputed leaders of naval warfare, another city-state claimed the best land force: Sparta. Sparta was renowned for its military strength, prowess, and sheer grit. Spartans were the elite of Greek warriors, and their entire society was centered on maintaining that power.

In Sparta, service to the state trumped the rights, freedoms, or comforts of the individual citizen. The Spartans valued strength above all else. Murder, cruelty, and thievery were all tolerated, and even encouraged, if they were necessary to remain strong. The Spartan soldiers' reputation was legendary throughout Greece, and their red cloaks—to hide blood—and long, wild hair instilled fear in the hearts of their enemies.

At birth, the elders of the society examined a child to determine if he or she was physically fit. Those who didn't pass were left to die. Even girls engaged in some military training, a quality unique to Sparta, but it was boys who bore the main responsibility. At age seven, a Spartan boy said good-bye to his family and went to live with other boys in a communal barracks to undergo his military preparation. During training, the boys received minimal clothing, one blanket, and only a little food. To keep from going hungry, they were encouraged to steal food—as long as they didn't get caught. At age 18, boys completed their training and joined the military. Boys who did not successfully finish training were not permitted to become full citizens. After finishing their training, men could marry, but they were still not allowed to live with their wives, a privilege that didn't come until they were 30. Sparta's system was rigorous and ruthless, but it paid off: Sparta possessed the finest soldiers in Greece.

A NEW WAY OF FIGHTING

The citizen-armies of hoplites, united under a city-state, characterized the Greek military for centuries. But the 300s BCE brought a revolution when Alexander the Great came into power.

The Helots

Sparta ruled over its neighboring lands and enslaved the residents. These people, called Helots, were forced to work the land, taking charge of agriculture and providing the Spartans with food. This system had an important benefit: it freed up the Spartans for military training. The Spartans treated the Helots brutally, however, and thus the ruling class lived under the constant threat of a slave revolt. To keep them in check, once a year the Spartans declared war on the Helots. They sought out those considered to be particularly dangerous and killed them. Because it was done as an act of war, the Spartans felt it did not qualify as murder.

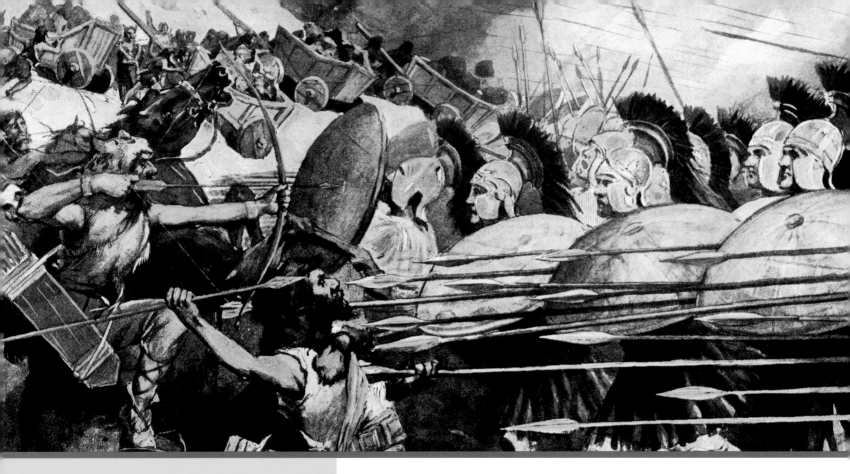

Alexander's armies wielded deadly power.

Alexander, who came from the northern region of Macedon, was the definition of a brilliant general, but he was also a merciless leader. Alexander had inherited his position from his father, Philip II, who had already begun changing the Greek style of warfare.

Although Spartan society was characterized by its constant attention to war, most Greek fighting fell around the other rhythms of life, such as planting and harvesting. But Philip, and after him Alexander, fought year round in all conditions. They built massive, professional armies that included any man who could wield a weapon. They were constantly at war, plundering the conquered to pay for more war. With sheer numbers on its side, Macedon began bringing the Greek city-states, one by one, under its control. Alexander's approach to war was absolutely ruthless: thousands were killed, including women and children. Property, buildings, and entire cities were destroyed. Torture and gleeful killing were normal under Alexander's reign. The golden age ended with Alexander, but not even his brutal style could erase the centuries of thought and development that would continue to influence Greek culture.

CHAPTER 9

THE GREEK LEGACY

From generation to generation, the Greeks passed down knowledge and refined their culture. They created new ways of thinking and found new things to think about. The foundations laid in ancient Greece became the basis for much of Western civilization. However, everything could have been lost had Greek civilization ended before its greatest achievements.

A frieze from the Temple of Athena Nike in Athens likely commemorates the Greek victory over the Persians at Marathon.

The turning point might have been that day in August, in 490 BCE, at the Battle of Marathon.

IF PERSIA HAD WON

The odds were stacked against the Athenians at Marathon, but some combination of luck and skill handed them a victory against the Persians. The Greek soldiers would live to fight another day, but more important, their way of life would survive and flourish. In fact, it might have been the victory itself that helped inspire the Greeks. The British historian Edward Creasy, who lived in the 1800s, observed, "[Marathon] broke forever the spell of Persian invincibility, which had paralyzed men's minds. . . . It secured for mankind the intellectual treasures of Athens, the growth of free institutions, [and] the liberal enlightenment of the Western world."[1] Had Persia been the victor, events might have played out much differently.

The victory at Marathon was more than a lucky break for the Greeks. It was also a lucky break for the future of Western civilization. Greece barely escaped extinction at a critical time, for it was on the cusp of making major breakthroughs in politics, philosophy, and science. Democracy, which was still in its infancy in the early 400s BCE, was allowed to grow and thrive, and future democracies would use the Athenian model to draw from. Democracy's influence went well beyond politics. Its ideals of freedom encouraged the development of Greek theater, art, and literature. Its principles flowed through the minds of philosophers and scientists.

The Greeks showed the world how public works could produce magnificent results when Pericles's massive building project produced the majestic Parthenon. They showed it how ingenuity could come in large packages and small, such as Archimedes's simple yet invaluable screw. The legacy the Greeks went on to leave after Marathon showed the results that come from a combination of confidence and optimism.

INTO ROME

Alexander, in attempting to spread the reach of Greece, had perhaps spread it too thin. The golden age of classical Greece had ended. Hellenistic Greeks made great artistic and scientific achievements, but Greece was in decline, and Rome was the rising star. By the beginning of the 200s BCE, Rome had begun skirmishing with the Greeks, in large part to keep the Macedon

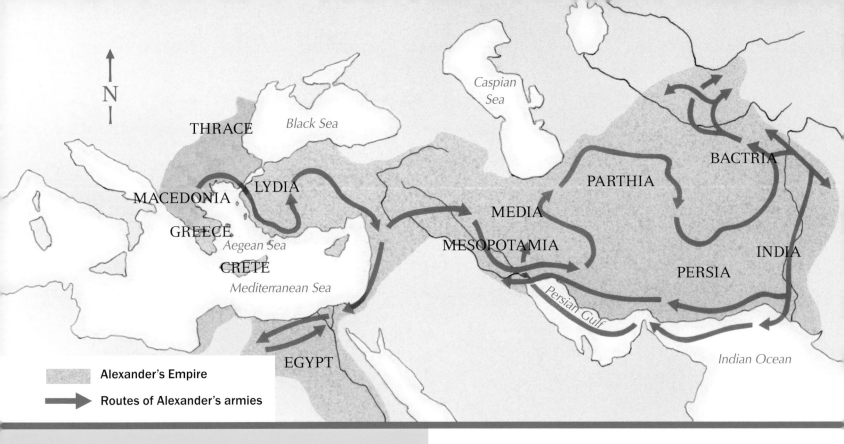

THRACE

Black Sea

*Caspian
Sea*

MACEDONIA

LYDIA

BACTRIA

PARTHIA

GREECE

MEDIA

Aegean Sea

MESOPOTAMIA

CRETE

INDIA

Mediterranean Sea

PERSIA

Persian Gulf

EGYPT

Indian Ocean

N

	Alexander's Empire
➤	Routes of Alexander's armies

Alexander's empire stretched across the Near East, but it
quickly fragmented after his death.

Empire from expanding farther. For the next 50 years, Roman military power
proved superior. The Romans would dismantle Alexander's empire and do
what the Persians never could: overtake Greece, securing their dominance
with the Battle of Corinth in 146.

Greece and Rome took vastly different approaches to building and maintaining an empire. The Romans valued order and discipline, and those qualities gave them the strength and resources to build their formidable power. However, it came at the expense of more creative pursuits. The Greeks, on the other hand, so taken with art and ideas, neglected the administrative and military requirements of empire building. The meeting of these societies, unsurprisingly, did not always go smoothly. As historians know from reading ancient sources, the Greeks felt they were better educated and better prepared to deal with intellectual challenges. They resented the Romans and their military might.

However, many Romans studied with Greek tutors, and their subsequent art, architecture, and literature echoed Greek influences. In the first century BCE, the Roman poet Horace wrote, "When Greece was taken she took control of her rough invader / and brought the arts to rustic Latium [Rome]."[2] In fact, much of the art and ideas the Greeks gave Western society does not come directly from them but rather filtered through the Romans.

MODERN REVIVAL

The Hellenistic Age closed with the end of the Roman Republic in 31 BCE. The Roman empire eventually fractured and divided in the 400s CE. The Western Roman Empire split into several small regions, although the

The Elgin Marbles

In the early 1800s, Lord Elgin, the British ambassador to the Ottoman Empire, visited the Parthenon. At the time, the Ottomans of Turkey controlled Greece. The structure was badly damaged, and Lord Elgin took many of its remaining statues and artifacts before they were destroyed. The decision was controversial. Some accused him of looting the Parthenon for his own personal gain or said he obtained the sculptures illegally. Later, upon his return to England, he sold the sculptures—called the Elgin Marbles—to the British Museum. Greece asked for them back years later, at the end of the 1900s. The British Museum said no, and a debate still rages over who should have possession of the marbles.

Eastern Roman Empire, centered in Constantinople, survived. Many citizens spoke Greek, and thus the Greek heritage remained, if somewhat submerged. Greek culture also survived via the Arab cultures that preserved ancient texts and built upon Greek science.

The Renaissance—a grand revival of arts, culture, and thinking in Europe—began in the 1300s CE in Italy, bringing with it a new appreciation of ideas. The Italians were anxious to learn about and in many cases imitate their ancient culture. The Italians had descended from the Romans, and much of what was Roman was also Greek. The ancient Greeks provided a natural source of inspiration.

By the 1700s, Europeans were beginning to travel to Greece. They returned with descriptions of the land and drawings of the magnificent architecture that still stood 2,000 years later. Scholars showed revived interest in the ancient texts of the Greek writers, and a study of the classics was the hallmark of a quality education. Several countries in Europe

Modern tourists travel from far and wide to visit ancient Greek sites.

also competed to snap up Greek artifacts and install them in national museums to prove their appreciation of Greek culture, and ancient Greek architectural styles were emulated in new buildings.

From architecture to math to democracy, today's scholars still chronicle the contributions of the ancient Greeks, debate their significance, and marvel at their ingenuity. Two millennia later, ancient Greece remains a fascinating place.

TIMELINE

1400 BCE–1100 BCE
The Mycenaean civilization thrives.

1100 BCE–800 BCE
Greece is in its Dark Age.

800 BCE–479 BCE
Greek society rebounds during
the Archaic Age.

776 BCE
The first Olympic Games are held.

700 BCE
The poet Homer composes the
Iliad and the *Odyssey*.

650 BCE–520 BCE
The Ionian Enlightenment occurs,
with influential thinkers such
as Thales and Pythagoras.

508 BCE
Cleisthenes introduces dramatic
democratic reforms in Athens.

490 BCE
Athens defeats Persia at the
Battle of Marathon.

480 BCE
Persia defeats the Greeks at Thermopylae;
the Greeks defeat Persia at Salamis.

479–320 BCE
Greek society flourishes
during the Classical Age.

447 BCE
Construction begins on the Parthenon.

431 BCE
The Peloponnesian War begins.

428 BCE
The influential philosopher Plato is born.

404 BCE
Sparta defeats Athens to end the Peloponnesian War.

336 BCE
Alexander becomes king of Macedon.

323 BCE
Alexander dies and the Hellenistic era begins.

200s BCE
Euclid writes *The Elements*.

290 BCE
The influential mathematician and scientist Archimedes is born.

146 BCE
Rome conquers Corinth.

1300s CE
Greek culture experiences a revival during the Italian Renaissance.

ANCIENT HISTORY

KEY DATES

- c. 1400 BCE–1100 BCE: Mycenaean civilization

- c. 800–479 BCE: Archaic Age

- 479–323 BCE: Classical Age

- 323–31 BCE: Hellenistic Age

KEY TOOLS AND TECHNOLOGIES

- The Greeks mastered the techniques of metalworking, forging bronze into vessels, statues, jewelry, tools, weapons, and armor.

- Catapults, levers, cranes, and pulleys were important machines used in war and in building.

- Hammers, chisels, and carving devices used for building stone and marble structures and statues likely were superior in quality compared with today's tools.

- The Greeks built what is considered the first computer, the Antikythera Mechanism, in the 100s BCE.

LANGUAGES

A language called Linear B, used by the Mycenaeans, was an early form of the Greek I language. In approximately 800 BCE, the Greeks adopted the Phoenician alphabet, which only had consonants, and they added vowels. This evolved into modern Greek and is the basis for other alphabets.

THE OLYMPIAN GODS & GODDESSES

APHRODITE – **Goddess of Love and Beauty**

APOLLO – **God of Light, Music, and Prophecy**

ARES – **God of War**

ARTEMIS – **Goddess of the Moon and the Hunt**

ATHENA – **Goddess of Wisdom and War**

HADES – **God of the Underworld**

HEPHAESTUS – **God of Fire and Forge**

HERA – **Queen of the Gods**

HERMES – **Messenger of the Gods**

HESTIA – **Goddess of Hearth and Home**

POSEIDON – **God of the Sea**

ZEUS – **King of the Gods**

IMPACT OF THE GREEK CIVILIZATION

- Early forms of democracy practiced in Athens and other city-states emphasized popular rights and were the catalyst for modern democracies.

- The Greeks valued thinking and philosophy as a fundamental part of human existence. The ideas explored by early Greek philosophers, particularly during the Classical Age, are still discussed today.

- Scientists emphasized observation and rational explanation, the underpinnings of today's scientific traditions.

- Greek styles of drama, literature, art, and architecture profoundly impacted the development of Western culture as they spread through Rome and beyond.

QUOTE

"Future ages will wonder at us, as the present age wonders at us now."

—Pericles

GLOSSARY

arable
Suitable for farming or agriculture.

aristocracy
A type of government formed of members from a noble class, with inherited power.

autonomous
Independent, self-sufficient.

barracks
Dormitories for soldiers that house many people.

coup
An act of seizing power from an unwilling leader or government.

homogenous
Characterized by being very similar.

invincibility

The state of being unable to be conquered or overcome.

oligarchy

A type of government formed by members of an elite, wealthy class.

oracle

A person believed able to communicate with the gods and relay their advice or messages.

symposium

A social gathering for men.

zenith

The point in time at which something reaches the height of its power.

ADDITIONAL RESOURCES

SELECTED BIBLIOGRAPHY

Cahill, Thomas. *Sailing the Wine-Dark Sea: Why the Greeks Matter*. New York: Doubleday, 2003. Print.

Garland, Robert. *Ancient Greece: Everyday Life in the Birthplace of Western Civilization*. New York: Sterling, 2008. Print.

Rodgers, Nigel. *The Rise and Fall of Ancient Greece*. London: Lorenz, 2008. Print.

FURTHER READINGS

Hunt, Norman Bancroft, ed. *Living In Ancient Greece*. New York: Chelsea, 2008. Print.

Marcovitz, Hal. *Ancient Greece (Understanding World History)*. San Diego: ReferencePoint, 2012. Print.

Nardo, Don. *Greenhaven Encyclopedia of Ancient Greece*. Farmington Hills: Greenhaven, 2006. Print.

WEBSITES

To learn more about Ancient Civilizations, visit **booklinks.abdopublishing.com**. These links are routinely monitored and updated to provide the most current information available.

PLACES TO VISIT

THE ACROPOLIS MUSEUM

15 Dionysiou Areopagitou Street

Athens, Greece 11742

+30 210 9000900

http://www.theacropolismuseum.gr/en

Opened in 2007, the new Acropolis Museum holds the treasures of ancient Athens.

THE METROPOLITAN MUSEUM OF ART

1000 Fifth Avenue

New York, NY 10028

212-535-7710

http://www.metmuseum.org

The Metropolitan Museum of Art holds a large and significant collection of ancient Greek art.

SOURCE NOTES

Chapter 1. A Crossroads of Cultures

1. Charles Freeman. *The Greek Achievement: The Foundation of the Western World.* New York: Penguin, 1999. Print. 23.

Chapter 2. On Mediterranean Shores

1. Nigel Rodgers. *The Rise and Fall of Ancient Greece.* London: Lorenz, 2008. Print. 42.

2. Ibid.

3. Victor Davis Hanson. *Wars of the Ancient Greeks.* Washington, DC: Smithsonian, 2004. Print. 174.

Chapter 3. Citizens and Slaves

1. Charles Freeman. *Egypt, Greece and Rome: Civilizations of the Ancient Mediterranean.* New York: Oxford UP, 1996. Print. 251.

2. Charles Freeman. *The Greek Achievement: The Foundation of the Western World.* New York: Penguin, 1999. Print. 121.

3. Ibid. 1.

4. Nigel Rodgers. *The Rise and Fall of Ancient Greece.* London: Lorenz, 2008. Print. 93.

5. Charles Freeman. *Egypt, Greece and Rome: Civilizations of the Ancient Mediterranean.* New York: Oxford UP, 1996. Print. 174.

6. Thomas R. Martin. *Ancient Greece: From Prehistoric to Hellenistic Times.* New Haven, CT: Yale UP, 1996. Print. 74.

7. Paul Lewis. "A Greek Treasure in France." *New York Times.* New York Times, 1 Apr. 1984. Web. 8 Aug. 2014.

Chapter 4. Daily Life

1. Robert Garland. *Ancient Greece: Everyday Life in the Birthplace of Western Civilization.* New York: Sterling, 2008. Print. 78.

2. Ibid. 135.

Chapter 5. Ideas and Ideals

1. Stephen Instone. "The Olympics: Ancient Versus Modern." *BBC History.* BBC, 17 Feb. 2011. Web. 8 Aug. 2014.

2. Ibid.

3. Justin Marozzi. *The Way of Herodotus: Travels with the Man Who Invented History.* Cambridge, MA: Da Capo, 2008. Print. 10.

4. Charles Freeman. *The Greek Achievement: The Foundation of the Western World.* New York: Penguin, 1999. Print. 242.

5. Douglas Linder. "The Trial of Socrates." *Famous Trials.* University of Missouri-Kansas City School of Law, 2002. Web. 8 Aug. 2014.

Chapter 6. In Service to the Gods

None.

SOURCE NOTES CONTINUED

Chapter 7. The First Scientists

None.

Chapter 8. Military Muscle

1. Victor Davis Hanson. *Wars of the Ancient Greeks*. Washington, DC: Smithsonian, 2004. Print. 33.

2. Thomas R. Martin. *Ancient Greece: From Prehistoric to Hellenistic Times*. New Haven, CT: Yale UP, 1996. Print. 62.

3. Joyce E. Salisbury. *Encyclopedia of Women in the Ancient World*. Santa Barbara, CA: ABC-CLIO, 2001. 83. *Google Book Search*. Web. 8. Aug. 2014.

Chapter 9. The Greek Legacy

1. Richard A. Billows. *Marathon: How One Battle Changed Western Civilization*. New York: Overlook Duckworth, 2010. Print. 46.

2. Horace. *The Satires of Horace and Perseus*. New York: Penguin, 1973. 179. *Google Book Search*. Web. 8 Aug. 2014.

INDEX

ABOUT THE AUTHOR

Diane Bailey has written approximately 40 nonfiction books for teens on topics including sports, celebrities, government, finance, and technology. Her personal favorite is anything to do with history, whether ancient Greece, medieval Europe, or Civil War–era America. Diane also works as a freelance editor. She has two sons and two dogs, and she lives in Kansas.